Forbidden Secrets of the

Illuminati

The Luciferian Deception

I0116200

Michael Adair

First Edition

Auriga Books
Edmonds, Washington

Adair, Michael. *Forbidden Secrets of the Illuminati: The Luciferian Deception.*

Copyright © 2019 by Cynthia Hodges, J.D., LL.M., M.A.

ISBN-10: 0-9763920-1-1
ISBN-13: 978-0-9763920-1-9

Published in the United States by
Auriga Books
Edmonds, Washington

Cover Art:
Back By PEAK99 - Own work, CC BY 3.0, https://commons.wikimedia.org/w/index.php?curid=75925621.

Contents

▲

Introduction

The Illuminati form a secret society that intends to destroy the *Ancient Régime* and impose the New World Order — an electronic meritocracy — in its stead. If they succeed in their plans, the only religion that will be permitted in their sphere of influence — which they aim to be the entire world — is their pagan Luciferian religion. This book reveals carefully guarded secrets of the society.

In an effort to recruit the author, who has familial connections to the Knights Templar and the Knights of Malta, an Illuminati grandmaster entrusted him with a secret manual. The text contains information that only members of the innermost circles of the Order are supposed to see. The Illuminati insider who leaked the manuscript instructed the author to write a pro-Illuminati book to help attract new members. Instead, the author has done quite the opposite, divulging details they did *not* want disclosed. He thereby hopes to warn people of the dangers of joining the Illuminati's ranks.

Unsuspecting recruits are often lured by the mystery surrounding the secret society and the promise of discovering forbidden secrets. In a three-phase indoctrination process, initiates are slowly acclimated to the Illuminati's belief system. The grandmasters skillfully transition them from a belief in God to the worship of Lucifer. The author hopes to foil this scheme by exposing the process the grandmasters use on students.

The shocking and disturbing culmination of the Illuminati agenda is only revealed to the initiates if they make it to the highest degrees of the mystery school. This book acts as a spoiler, as it exposes what is really occurring in such "sacred" occult rituals as the Merkaba Hexagram Ceremony.

The contents of the secret manual that was delivered to the author were compiled from various sources, including reference texts that are only available to Illuminati grandmasters. In an effort to maintain intellectual integrity to the greatest extent possible, some of the information has been tracked down to the following sources:

Hockney, Michael. *The Armageddon Conspiracy*. USA: Lulu.com, 2008.

Lederman, Leon M. *The God Particle: If the Universe Is the Answer, What Is the Question?* USA: Delta, 1994.

Mathers, Samuel Liddell Macgregor. *The Greater Key of Solomon*. USA: Theophania Publishing, 2010.

Mathers, Samuel Liddell Macgregor. *The Goetia: The Lesser Key of Solomon the King: Lemegeton - Clavicula Salomonis Regis, Book 1*. USA: Red Wheel, 2011.

Wilson, Robert Anton. *The Illuminati Papers*. USA: Ronin Publishing, 1997.

Unfortunately, the following references were named in the secret manual, but no further information is available about them at the time of publication:

The Seven Books of Divine Knowledge
Dark Secrets of the Illuminati
The Ancient Pathway to Wisdom
The Illuminati Chronicles
Solomon and the Order of Light
The Genesis Singularity
The Divine Keys of Supreme Revelation

An *Interview with a Grandmaster of the Order of Light: transcript of an interview with Prince Leo Zagami, Grandmaster of the P2 Lodge* was also referenced, but no other specifics can be obtained.

The author consulted with a Witch High Priest who defected from the Order and interviewed an Illuminati grandmaster extensively while writing this book to ensure the accuracy of the information contained herein.

The Luciferian Deception

The members of the Illuminati comprise a secret society that descends from the ancient Brotherhood of the Snake. The Brotherhood was an occult religious order that is said to date back to the days of the Garden of Eden.

The Brotherhood worshipped Lucifer and rejected Yahweh, aka Jehovah. The Brotherhood venerated Lucifer because they believed that he generously shared occult knowledge with mankind. Yahweh, on the other hand, jealously withheld such information. Yahweh refused to share wisdom with humans so as to keep them in the dark, as this made them easier to control. Because of this history, the Illuminati are opposed to any religion that worships Yahweh and rejects Lucifer. They are especially hostile to the Abrahamic religions, namely Christianity, Judaism, and Islam. Illuminists seek to obliterate these faiths and their followers.

The Illuminati aspire to destroy the free nation states of the *Ancient Régime* (Old World Order) and force an electronic meritocracy christened the New World Order onto all of the people of the world. They plan to consolidate power in their own hands and exert global domination by means of a one world government. In the New World Order, no religion will be tolerated save their Luciferian religion. In other words, everyone will be forced to worship Lucifer and accept him as "God."

To accomplish their goals of global dominance, the Illuminati hope to recruit people of power, wealth, and influence. To that end, they target politicians, corporate leaders, captains of industry, global bankers, as well as the best and brightest scientific minds. These people serve to further the society's agenda through their connections, knowledge, and financial resources.

To counter any initial resistance to their aspirations and creed, the Illuminati engage in deception. They reveal their Luciferian belief system gradually in stages. The initiates are only told the truth about the Luciferian agenda once they reach the higher degrees of the Order. By that time, they are completely brainwashed by Illuminism.

By withholding crucial information from the new recruits, the grandmasters create a sense of mystery. They leverage this mystery to lure desired initiates into their fold. A member who has attained a higher degree is sworn to secrecy and forbidden from disclosing his or her knowledge to a lower-ranked student. A violation of this oath could result in a gruesome death, described as having one's throat cut, one's tongue torn out by its roots, and one's "body buried in the rough sands of the sea at low water mark." Threats and fear ensure secrecy amongst the members.

When a new student enters the first phase of initiation, the grandmaster tells him or her that the Illuminati believe in God and are trying to "bring the light of truth to the world." The grandmaster discusses cosmology, such as how the Grand Creator made the dual universe of mind and matter. He skillfully couches the pagan religion in scientific terms to lend it credibility. This machination is especially geared towards drawing in the more scientifically- and rationally-minded individuals.

During the first phase, the student is introduced to the *Demiurge* (which will later turn out to be none other than Satan). As it is explained, this malevolent creature invaded Earth eons ago. Ever since its first appearance, the *Demiurge* has been trying to capture the hearts and minds of humans. This being is determined to ensnare people in eternal darkness and damnation. To that end, this evil entity has deceived people into following false religions. Doing so leads them away from the Light of Truth, which provides a means of escape from its domination.

After striking fear into the heart of the student, the grandmaster will reassure him or her that the Illuminati are trying to destroy the *Demiurge* and free humanity from ignorance, despair, and slavery. The Illuminati grandmaster, Adam Weishaupt, claimed that

> [t]he Illuminati's noble and historic mission is to release man's higher self by destroying the archons — the princes of the world — who prosecute Satan's will and hold mankind in their thrall.

The fear instilled in the initiates is meant to induce them to cling to the pagan Luciferian religion for protection from the invisible threat posed by the terrifying *Demiurge*.

In the next stage of indoctrination, the grandmaster will tell the student that God is really a cosmic being called *Abraxas*, which means the Giver of Wisdom and Light. *Abraxas* created the universe in the Big Bang. Illuminists claim they are working towards proving *Abraxas'* existence through science. This is meant to bolster the pagan religion with scientific credentials.

If an initiate successfully moves up the ranks to the third phase, the grandmaster will reveal the carefully guarded secret that Lucifer is God. According to their tenets, Lucifer brings truth, light, and wisdom to the human race. He is supposedly the only one who can save humanity from Satan's clutches.

The grandmasters of the Order are careful to withhold information about Lucifer from the students in the earlier stages of indoctrination. They wait until the initiates have been primed and are ready to receive such knowledge. If a student plans to progress further up the ladder in the society, he or she must accept that Lucifer is God as being the ultimate Truth. *Abraxas* is exposed as merely having been a transitional figure used to draw initiates away from a belief in God and toward the worship of Lucifer.

The following chapters go into more detail about the Illuminati's three-phase process that leads students from believing in God at the beginning to glorifying Lucifer at the end. In the last phase, perhaps the most carefully hidden secret is revealed, which is how the Illuminists use occult rituals to summon demons to do their bidding.

▲

Phase I
Genesis and
"False" Religions

In Phase I of the initiation process into the secret society, the grandmaster will claim that the Illuminati believe in God, and hope to enlighten humanity by bringing "the light of truth to the world." To further that goal, the use of reason is extolled, as per Adam Weishaupt: "G [God] is Grace, the Flaming Star is the Torch of Reason. Those who possess this knowledge are indeed Illuminati." Those people who take religious beliefs on faith are dismissed as being "irrational."

The grandmaster will elucidate on cosmology and discuss how the Great Architect created the dual universe of mind and matter. The Genesis creation myth is phrased in scientific terms to make it more persuasive, and is described in the following paragraphs.

In the beginning, God was the only thing that existed. This creative force did not exist in physical space, but rather existed outside of space and time as pure thought and absolute Mind. He wielded infinite power and infinite spiritual and intellectual energy, but was completely alone in the void.

At some point, God decided to transform Himself from pure Mind into matter. Such a transformation meant the death of pure Mind and the birth of matter infused with Mind. In so doing, God hoped to gain complete knowledge of existence, because he realized that consciousness requires interaction with otherness to develop. Illuminati grandmaster, Georg Wilhelm Friedrich Hegel, explained that

> [t]he divine idea is just this, to disclose itself, to posit the Other outside itself and to take it back again into itself in order to be subjectivity and mind/spirit.

God needed to create otherness by externalizing Himself, or in other words, by creating consciousness outside and beyond Himself to become self-actualized.

To that end, God declared, "Let there be Life!" In a demonstration of infinite power, intellectual curiosity, and courage, He self-immolated in the explosive Big Bang event. In that instant 14 billion years ago, God created the physical universe of matter out of nothing but pure Mind. During that split-second phase of what physicists call "inflation," the matter required to create countless stars and planets materialized literally out of thin air.

Due to its origins, physical matter is a form of energy that is infused with God's Mind. To put it another way, matter is Mind with physical dimensions. Mind and matter are two aspects of the same substance (i.e. two sides of the same coin). Matter exists in dimensional space, while Mind is non-dimensional and exists outside of space and time. At the most fundamental level, time, space, energy, matter, particle, and wave are all the same substance simply viewed from different perspectives. The Greek philosopher, Empedocles, attempted to capture this concept by asserting, "God is a circle whose center is everywhere, and its circumference nowhere."

After proffering a reasonably scientific-sounding creation myth, the grandmaster sets about discrediting "false" religions to further the agenda of promoting their Luciferian religion. The Illuminati attack the Abrahamic religions especially so as to undermine adherents' faith in the God of competing creeds.

According to the Illuminati's teachings, the intent of the *Demiurge* is to prevent humans from entering the Light of Truth and Knowledge, and thereby enslave them in eternal darkness. Illuminists claim that the diabolical *Demiurge* (Satan) is really the "God" of the Torah, Bible, and Koran. Therefore, anyone who follows one of the Abrahamic religions has been deceived by the Devil into believing a false religion — and is really worshipping Satan.

By convincing initiates that the God of competing religions is actually Satan, the grandmasters separate the student from their God as they had previously known Him. They also create division between people, because followers of Abrahamic faiths are "devil-worshippers." This is, in effect, a divide and conquer strategy.

The attack on the Abrahamic religions begins with the grandmaster condemning Judaism, as it was the first to appear in history. According to the Illuminati's tenets, Jehovah (or Yahweh) is a God designed by and for the Jews. This God aligns Himself with His Chosen People in a partisan fashion rather than lending his support to all of the people in His creation equally. Jehovah enters into sacred covenants — legally binding contracts — only with the Jews. He allocates land that just happens to be inhabited by other people to His Chosen Ones. Jehovah helped His favorites attack and slaughter gentiles in the Promised Land of Canaan. He even went so far as to drown the entire world in the Great Flood, sparing only a precious few in Noah's Ark.

The grandmaster will point out that, despite the Jews' most favored person status with "God," they have endured millennia of ill-treatment at the hands of goyim. The genocide and associated horrors of the Holocaust were perhaps the apex of the persecution against Jehovah's "Chosen People."

The paradox of the Chosen Ones suffering such injustices is meant to cause the student to question whether there is any rational basis for believing that Yahweh is a "good" God. The implication is that the Old Testament God is a primitive, savage, tribal God prone to cruelty and violence.

The grandmaster will further accuse this "god" of sowing suspicion, confusion and division among people of different cultures. Such behavior is pointed out as being characteristic of *Satan*, not God. To support this argument, the grandmaster will cite the Gnostics of Biblical times, who likewise believed that Jehovah was really Satan.

Islam will also be ruthlessly denounced. The Koran will be condemned as being ambiguous and muddled despite proclaiming to be the divine word of Allah. Islam will be further discredited by the grandmaster as being a violent religion, despite followers' insistence that it is a peaceful religion. The grandmaster will draw attention to the fact that

Islam was forced on people of different cultures via *jihad* — holy war — rather than winning devotees by peaceful means.

To bolster their argument, the Illuminati grandmaster will point out that a brutal and illiterate warrior, Mohammed, was chosen to receive the Koran by the angel, Gabriel. In Socratic fashion, the student will be asked why Allah needed an intermediary and why Allah did not just telepathically transmit the words to Mohammed Himself. Further, why did Allah not just choose a person who could write, rather than pick the illiterate Mohamed and force him to memorize the entire text of the Koran, and then tediously recite it to scribes? Drawing attention to such inconsistencies is, in part, meant to lead the student to the conclusion that Islam is, in fact, a religion of conquest, tailor-made to serve certain interests.

The third and final Abrahamic religion to be vilified is Christianity. Jesus Christ (aka Yehoshua ben Yosef) was — according to Christian orthodoxy — a unique incarnation of God on Earth, being both the Son of God and God Himself. This Christian God could have chosen to incarnate anywhere on Earth, where He could have proclaimed a new, non-partisan, universal religion of peace, love, and compassion. Instead, He chose to incarnate in Israel as a Jew. As a result, Christians may celebrate the New Testament, but they are forced to accept the Old Testament at the same time. Thus, they are also unwittingly worshipping Satan. As part of the tactic to undermine the Christian faith, the grandmaster reveals the "true" history of Jesus Christ to the eager student.

At the time when Judah chafed under the yoke of the Roman occupation, the Jews longed to be free. They dreamed of reuniting the southern kingdom of Judah with the northern kingdom of Israel to form the united kingdom of Israel as it existed at the time of King David.

The Jesus Plot, which was alluded to in the Gospels, was a scheme to restore the Rex Deus (Latin for "King God") family of priest-kings to the throne of Israel. This family is also referred to as the Star Family because they have sought esoteric astrological and astronomical knowledge via the occult.

The Star Family traces its ancestry to David, King of Israel, of the royal tribe of Judah, and to Aaron of the priestly

Levi tribe (first high priest of the Ark of the Covenant and brother of Moses). Based on the two famous ancestors, the family professes to combine the sacred and the secular, the divine and the earthly powers into a single family bloodline.

By the time of Jesus' thirtieth birthday, it had been over 600 years since a monarch of the line of David had reigned in Jerusalem. To restore a Davidic king to the throne, the Romans would have to be driven out of Judah. Such a feat would require a national insurrection. As Jesus (of the Rex Deus family) did not believe that the Roman war machine could be defeated by guerrilla tactics, a strategy was devised to make the occupation of Judah so costly that the Romans would cut their losses and leave of their own accord.

The inspiration for the nation to rise up against the Romans was to be a human Ark of the Covenant. The Ark of the Covenant had been the holy vessel that had contained the *Shekinah*, the earthly presence of Yahweh. In the days of Joshua, the Jewish priests would carry the Ark of the Covenant into battle. Yahweh's presence was meant to ensure that the enemies of Israel would be vanquished.

The leaders of the Davidic royal family sought a special person to be the human vessel for the *Shekinah*. This person would be the flesh and blood container of Yahweh, and give voice to the Divine. Jesus, being of the line of David, was chosen to be this human Ark of the Covenant. He was to be the manifestation of God on Earth.

The myth of Jesus Christ was constructed so as to establish his divine credentials. He was said to have been born of a virgin to set his birth apart from that of ordinary mortals. To show that Jesus was a king, three wise men travelled from the East bearing valuable gifts, namely gold, frankincense, and myrrh, to present to him. The shepherds visiting Jesus in his manger showed that he was still a humble man of the people. The star that burned brightly over Bethlehem at the time of Jesus' birth was the symbol of the Star (Rex Deus) Family.

To prove that Jesus was God incarnate, he would have to do something miraculous — something impossible for mere mortals. It was decided that he would rise from the dead. As it is literally impossible to rise from the dead, a convincing ruse was arranged. A drug [perhaps a neurotoxin] was found that could induce a death-like state for a long enough period of time to convince anyone that the person in question was, in fact, bereft of life.

Jesus did a dry run of the "Resurrection Job" on his brother-in-law, Lazarus, brother of Mary Magdalene (as chronicled in the Gospel of John). When Lazarus "died," Jesus waited two days before he went to "raise him from the dead." He announced, "Lazarus our friend sleepeth, but I go that I may awake him out of sleep."

By the time Jesus arrived in Bethany, a small town just outside of Jerusalem, Lazarus had been "four days already in the grave." Jesus proclaimed to be "the resurrection and the life: he that believeth in me, although he be dead, shall live." Together, Jesus, Mary Magdalene, and Mary's sister, Martha, made their way to Lazarus' "tomb," which was really just a cave with a sizable stone laid across the entrance.

The drug Lazarus had taken to simulate death wore off after a day or so. By the time he had recovered from its effects, he was already in the tomb and left for dead. The Dearly Departed had planted a hidden supply of food and water in the cave prior to his "death" so that he could await Jesus' arrival without undue discomfort. When Jesus called upon Lazarus to "come forth," he did, "bound feet and hands with winding bands, and his face was bound about with a napkin."

Some of the Jews who had witnessed this "miracle" reported to the Pharisees what Jesus had done. The Sanhedrin, the supreme religious body, assembled to discuss the matter. They were suspicious of the "miracle worker." The Sanhedrin feared Jesus could spark a revolution that would bring the wrath of the Romans down upon their heads. Worried, they asked:

> What do we do? For this man doth many miracles. If we let him alone so, all will believe in him, and the Romans will come, and take away our place and nation.

In fact, according to the Illuminati, Jesus *was* the leader of an armed rebel force against the Jewish establishment and the Roman occupiers. He had even ordered his followers to sell their clothes so that they could buy weapons, directing, "He that hath no sword, let him sell his garment, and buy one."

Caiaphas, the Jewish high priest, understood what was at stake. He explained to the Sanhedrin that, "It is expedient for you that one man should die for the people, and that the whole nation perish not." Therefore, to quell the rebellion, the Sanhedrin "devised to put him [Jesus] to death."

Unbeknownst to the members of the Sanhedrin, there was a spy amongst them — Joseph of Arimathea. Their scribe was the brother of Jesus. Long before, a feud had been staged between Joseph and Jesus to make it seem as though their relationship had broken down irreparably. Joseph gained the trust of the administrative group that served the Sanhedrin, and was even consulted about Jesus' likely plans, movements, and whereabouts. However, Joseph was, in reality, fully committed to Jesus and the Star Family's agenda.

Joseph warned Jesus that the Sanhedrin had sentenced him to death. If caught, Jesus would be stoned to death. Therefore, Jesus

> walked no more openly amongst the Jews, but he went into a country near the desert, unto a city that is called Ephraim, and there he abode with his disciples.

In other words, Jesus and his army went into temporary hiding.

While Jerusalem was preparing to celebrate the great festival of the Passover, the whole of Judah was buzzing with excitement about how Jesus had raised Lazarus from the dead. The populous waited anxiously to see what Jesus would do next. It was widely believed that, if Jesus came to Jerusalem for the Passover, either the whole city would rise up and his military coup would succeed, or he would perish in the attempt. The Bible relates the events:

> And on the next day, a great multitude that was come to the festival day, when they had heard that Jesus was coming to Jerusalem, took branches of palm trees, and went forth to meet him, and cried, "Hosanna, blessed be

the King of Israel that cometh in the name of the Lord, peace in heaven and glory on high."

The Pharisees were appalled by Christ's rapturous reception, proclaiming in exasperation, "Do you see that we prevail nothing? Behold, the whole world it goes after him."

Jesus was being hailed as the true Messiah — the divinely-mandated and legitimate king. This was a direct challenge to Rome, as only the caesar could appoint kings. Far from disclaiming this exalted position, Jesus encouraged such sentiments. As the Bible recounts,

> And Jesus found a young ass, and sat upon it, as it is written,..."Fear not, daughter of Sion...behold, thy king cometh, sitting on an ass's colt."

Such exploits were considered by the authorities to be acts of high treason punishable by death.

A great crowd followed Jesus as he triumphantly entered the temple. Jesus confronted the Jewish establishment and their money system, as described in the Bible:

> And entering into the temple, he began to cast out them that sold therein, and them that bought, saying to them, "It is written, My house is the house of prayer. But you have made it a den of thieves."

Jesus seized control of the temple and began preaching to the people as a fiery demagogue, working them into a frenzy. A full-scale uprising seemed imminent.

The Roman and Jewish leaders met in an emergency session to decide what to do next. Pontius Pilate, the Roman governor of Judea, was not confident that he had enough men to deal with Jesus and his insurgents, so he sent for reinforcements.

Meanwhile, Jesus sensed that the situation was about to boil over. He gathered with his wife (Mary Magdalene), brother-in-law, brothers and other loyal disciples for a last supper. Jesus prepared them for his death and resurrection.

Only Lazarus was aware that Jesus would simply be repeating the "Resurrection Job" to which he had been a party.

The "traitor" was also chosen to complete Jesus' martyrdom scam. The person who would betray Jesus could not be James, because he had been tapped to be King of Israel after Jesus' "death." Neither would Simon Peter fill the bill, as he had been slated to be the high priest of the new Jewish church. Obviously, Joseph would not do, since he was a scribe to the Sanhedrin and was not a part of Jesus' entourage. Judas was finally selected to "betray" Jesus.

Ironically, Judas really *was* a traitor to Jesus. Judas had thrown in his lot with Simon Magus, leader of the Illuminati, and was leaking information to him about everything Jesus was up to. Judas later joined the inner circle of Simon Magus and wrote the Gospel of Judas, which is in the hands of the Illuminati to this day.

After the Last Supper, Jesus rejoined his rebel army on the Mount of Olives, accompanied by Lazarus and the other male attendees of the famous dinner party. Most of the rag-tag soldiers in the camp were asleep, resting prior to the dawn attack on Jerusalem. As it turned out, there would be no glorious battle.

Judas betrayed Jesus to the Sanhedrin, telling them of an unguarded path that led directly to the heart of the rebel camp. The Jews relayed this information to Pilate, who immediately assembled a Roman cohort (600 soldiers), accompanied by the Jewish temple guards. The cohort invaded the camp via the unguarded path as the insurgents slept, and took them by surprise. Jesus' soldiers put up a fierce fight and managed to briefly push the Romans back. In the fray, Jesus was struck across the forehead, which made it appear as though he were sweating blood. Some of Jesus' soldiers escaped, some were captured, but most surrendered. Many were crucified alongside their Messiah.

After a perfunctory trial, Pilate ordered Jesus' execution. Jesus was fastened to a cross alongside the insurrectionists who had fought with him.

To carry out the Resurrection Job, a man secretly working for Jesus had put the drug that Lazarus had taken into a vessel containing vinegar. After hanging on the cross for a few hours, Jesus cried out, "I thirst!" The man handed the container to Jesus for him to drink. The drug in the vinegar induced a death-like state in Jesus, just as it had done in Lazarus.

The Roman guards spared Jesus the agony of having his legs broken, which was sometimes done to crucifixion victims to hasten their death. Breaking their legs made it impossible for them to support their weight as it hung suspended on the cross. The weight of the body crushed their lungs, causing them to suffocate. It is unknown whether Jesus was really stabbed in the side by the Spear of Destiny as recounted in John 19:34, or whether this event was fabricated to dispel lingering doubts as to Jesus' death.

As it appeared that Jesus had departed this life within a few hours, when most crucifixion victims took two to three days to expire, Pilate was astonished and suspicious. However, the governor was preoccupied with restoring order to the city, so he handed the body over to Jesus' brother, Joseph. Truly believing Jesus to be dead, Joseph placed him in a tomb. Although Matthew claims that Pilate posted a guard at the entrance of the tomb (Matthew 27:62-66), it is doubtful that the governor had any soldiers to spare, as they would likely be needed to subdue the tumultuous city.

At this point, the Illuminati story takes an unexpected twist. They claim Jesus actually *did* die, but that his soul left his body and passed into a new "vessel." The body that became the new host for Jesus' soul belonged to a man who had hidden near the tomb in hopes of witnessing the miracle of Jesus' resurrection (recounted in Mark 14:51). This man got more than he bargained for.

Jesus' soul passed into the man lingering near the tomb and basically possessed this person. Jesus instantly became the dominant personality. This soul transfer supposedly accounts for why Jesus' appearance changed so drastically after the resurrection that even his closest friends and associates did not recognize him.

The original Star Family plan was to have Jesus parade around triumphantly, proving that he was God incarnate due to his miraculous resurrection from the dead. This was meant to inspire the Jewish people to rally behind their Messiah and oust the oppressive Roman occupation forces. After the Romans had been vanquished, Jesus was to provide the divine sanction for James to assume the throne and for Simon Peter to be anointed High Priest of the Temple. In this way, the Rex Deus family hoped to restore the Davidic monarchy of Israel and found a new religion that they would control as Jewish king-popes. Jesus would then "ascend to heaven" — leave the country — before anyone discovered he was a mere mortal and not really the human Ark of the Covenant.

This entire plan was now impossible because Jesus was no longer recognizable as being Jesus. Only those who knew him well were willing to believe that he had taken on a new body. Even Thomas doubted it was really Jesus. For the rest of the Jews, there was no reason to accept that he had done the impossible as he had promised to do. The Jesus Plot to restore the Rex Deus bloodline to power had failed.

The Star Family was forced to flee Judea, and chose to resettle in France. The new form of Judaism they concocted — Christianity — was still centered on Jesus Christ. However, they could hardly present Jesus as a Jewish Messiah of the Davidic line who had led an uprising against Rome. Jesus now had to be made acceptable to a Roman audience. Paul began the process by linking Jesus to Mithraism rather than to Judaism. For example, the birthday of Jesus, December 25, just happens to coincide with Mithra's birthday and, quite coincidentally, Lucifer's as well. It was this Romanized version of Christianity that gained a foothold in Europe.

Through this new religion, the Rex Deus family rose to prominence. From their bloodline sprang forth the Merovingian dynasty of France and the Stuarts of Scotland and England. The Star Family was also connected to the House of Habsburg, the Grand Ducal Family of Luxembourg, the Scottish clan Sinclair, and the House of Cavendish. Thus, this bloodline forms the core of the Power Elite. The *Demiurge* exploits their power, wealth, and influence to control the world.

After the three Abrahamic religions are trashed in the eyes of the initiate, the Illuminati begin Phase II of the indoctrination process, which includes establishing the scientific support for their pagan belief system.

Phase II
Genesis and Science

In Phase II of the Illuminati indoctrination, the grandmaster informs the student that God is really a cosmic being called *Abraxas*. This entity is the Giver of Wisdom and Light that created the universe in the Big Bang. The grandmaster claims that the Illuminati's goal is to prove *Abraxas*' existence through modern science. Thus, an appeal is made to scientific rationality to legitimize their pagan religion.

The elaborate scientific basis for the Luciferian religion begins at the center of a black hole — the singularity. The Illuminati assert that this is the key to understanding the nature of reality and the fundamental composition of the universe.

The singularity is a dimensionless point with zero radius and zero volume, yet infinite density and gravity. The physical universe collapses into the singularity, where time itself ceases to exist. The singularity is described mathematically as $r = 0$, where r is the distance from the black hole. The physical universe is described as $r > 0$.

The singularity exists outside of space and time. Any point that is not in space and time cannot be said to be located anywhere, since that would be a defined position in space. Thus, the singularity is everywhere and nowhere at the same time.

The singularity ($r = 0$) is the dimensionless, non-physical universe of mind, where thoughts and memories exist. The dream-state is the closest one can experience of the $r = 0$ domain. In dreams, there is no "hard" time or "hard" space.

The dimensional ($r > 0$) and the dimensionless ($r = 0$) aspects of the universe co-exist in a single continuum. The concept of co-existence is described mathematically as $r >= 0$.

The $r >= 0$ paradigm provides a framework for understanding the true nature of the universe, according to the Illuminati.

At the time of the Big Bang, the physical universe of matter exploded out of the dimensionless universe of mind ($r = 0$). Dimensionless energy was transformed into dimensional energy to create the physical universe of dimensions ($r > 0$). At the singularity of a black hole, dimensional energy is converted back into dimensionless energy. This flux between matter conversion creates a perpetual motion machine. The universe is, in effect, a perpetual motion machine, as it is continually converting dimensional energy into dimensionless energy, and back again.

Because the $r > 0$ physical domain is superimposed over the $r = 0$ domain, the domain of mind pervades the physical domain. The domain of mind is the aether (aka quintessence), which is an immaterial substance that permeates all matter. It is not in the physical domain, yet it is omnipresent in the physical domain. The aether breathes life into the physical domain, and is sometimes referred to as *pneuma*, the breath, spirit, or soul of *Abraxas*. Because mind permeates matter, the $r >= 0$ framework is *panpsychic*, meaning "all mind." In other words, everything — rocks, trees, air, sand, grass, water, etc. — is imbued with mind.

Although the world may appear to be based on locality, it is, in fact, based on an unmediated, unseen reality that permits faster than light — and probably instantaneous — communication.

The interaction between mind and matter can be illustrated using the EPR Paradox. This has to do with a phenomenon known as quantum entanglement involving pairs of correlated particles. For example, if the first particle in a pair has a certain property, such as spin that can be described as "up," then the other paired particle must have the opposite spin property of "down." The two spins effectively cancel each other out. If they did not, then spin asymmetry would develop, which would lead to instability.

According to classical physics, the two particles have opposite spin states from the outset. However, quantum theory holds that each particle exists in a superposition of the up and down spin states. In other words, neither particle has a clear-cut spin state. It is not until a measurement is carried out and the spin wave-function "collapses" that a particle can be said to have a definite spin state. This instantaneously causes the spin wave-function of the other particle to collapse into the opposite state.

The EPR Paradox concerns two particles separated by a great distance where no instantaneous communication between the two particles is possible within the paradigm of conventional physics. If one particle is measured to be "up," then how does the other particle know that its spin wave-function should collapse into the "down" state? What mechanism could be used to communicate such information? Illuminism claims to solve the EPR Paradox with the following explanation.

The pair of entangled particles exists both in the dimensional material universe and in the dimensionless mental universe. While they may be separated in the physical universe by a vast distance, they are still connected in the mental universe. No matter how far apart they are in physical space, they are permanently connected in the universe of mind. When a measurement is carried out on one, the outcome is immediately reflected in the mental universe. In turn, that result is immediately reflected in the paired particle located in the mental universe. As soon as the results of the measurement are known in the mental universe, they are immediately reflected in the physical universe.

With a new understanding of the mind-matter universe, psychic ability can be explained. Such powers are mediated by the dimensionless mental universe where time and space do not exist and everything is, in a sense, connected and whole. One may be able to perceive anything that is happening anywhere by tuning in to the dimensionless mind and using it to access the dimensional physical universe.

Illuminism teaches that the conscious and the unconscious mind together constitute the Mind at Large. The more one opens one's mind, i.e. expands one's consciousness into the unconscious, the more one enters into the $r = 0$ domain of the Mind of God. When the barrier between one's limited consciousness and the unlimited consciousness of God suddenly breaks down, one attains gnosis. Gnosis is the culmination of existence when one merges one's own mind with the Mind of God. At that point, one is not merely sharing God's thoughts, one *is* God. In effect, the Illuminati claim their religion is the path to actually becoming God.

After a seemingly plausible scientific explanation for their belief system, the Illuminati grandmaster informs the student that *Abraxas* is not the creator of the universe after all, but that the universe is actually creating God. This is because the physical universe is evolving towards its destiny, which is to reconstitute God in a new form of mind and matter. Therefore, God is not complete, pure, or perfect, but is merely in the process of becoming so.

Every particle of matter, regardless of how small or insignificant, is a spark of God. As with a hologram, each spark contains the whole (God), and the whole is comprised of each individual spark. As the Greek philosopher, Heraclitus, put it, "All things come out of the one, and the one out of all things."

The divine sparks that God manifested at the time of Creation, the Alpha Point, are traveling towards the Omega Point (end). The Omega Point is perfection. God is the end-point of evolution, but transcends evolution at the same time.

As the universe evolves, the cosmic mind attains greater control over the cosmic body, which is the physical universe. When the mind has full control of the "body," then the universe becomes God. At that point, God is the master of the universe and creation. *Abraxas* is in the unique position of being both the Creator of the universe and its creation. The universe cycles on forever in the process of always Becoming rather than simply existing in a static state of Being.

In Phase III of the initiation process, yet more surprises await the student of Illuminism. These include the fact that Lucifer is God and that the Illuminati invoke demonic entities known as Djinn in occult rituals. These "genies" are called upon to bestow secret knowledge and worldly power and riches upon them, but at a terrible price.

▲

Phase III
Lucifer Revealed

If an initiate is successful in ascending the Illuminati mystery school degrees, the grandmaster will disclose a carefully guarded secret in Phase III. The student is told about a cosmic being that *Abraxas* created, one that bestows truth, light and knowledge upon the human race. This being is revealed to be none other than Lucifer.

Lucifer is said to come from a higher dimensional plane and is credited with granting the Light of Truth to the Illuminists. Albert Pike, Illuminati grandmaster and the supreme grandmaster of the Freemasons, divulged that "Lucifer is God...the God of Light." Therefore, the Illuminati believe that Lucifer is God. They also think that Lucifer is the only one who can rescue humanity from Satan. Everything the student has been taught up to this point is, once again, turned upside down.

As the creation myth story continues, *Abraxas* created a dazzling realm fashioned from light, but nothing He had created thus far gave Him what He really needed. Because *Abraxas* wanted to become fully self-actualized, He needed to interact with an otherness comparable to Himself. To that end, *Abraxas* cloned Himself to create Lucifer, the Son of God. Lucifer soon longed for a brother to keep him company, so *Abraxas* cloned a second son. This son was named Paracletus, which means the "comforter" or "the one called to help." *Abraxas* showed both of his sons how to clone themselves, which they did. The clones the brothers created are known as angels. Each angel reflects the nature of its respective creator.

In the beginning, Paracletus was almost as luminous as Lucifer, but he was afflicted by doubts about himself and lacked self-esteem. Eventually, Paracletus suffered a crisis of identity and rejected the Light all together. At this point, he became "darkness visible," as the 17th century English poet and author, John Milton, phrased it. Paracletus eventually became known as Satan, which means "accuser" or "adversary."

Satan had originally been intended to be Lucifer's companion, but he was envious of his radiant brother. He was jealous of the relationship Lucifer enjoyed with their Father. Satan resented being the youngest and weakest of the three. He compensated by cultivating extreme pride. He even deluded himself into thinking he was superior to Lucifer and even to *Abraxas*. Satan refused to acknowledge that he had been created, but rather insisted that he had always existed. He even went so far as to declare himself to be omnipotent, omniscient, and perfect.

Satan's resentment eventually grew into hatred. Hatred led to rebellion. Satan and his minions took up arms against *Abraxas* and Lucifer. The battle that raged was furious, but Satan and his army were eventually defeated by the Angels of Light. Satan and his fallen angels were banished from God's realm. They were cast out into the gloomy darkness where the light of *Abraxas* had never penetrated.

After being ousted from God's universe, Satan created a rival sub-universe fashioned from matter rather than from light. Satan sarcastically announced the creation of this realm with the words, "Let there be light!" With that, Satan — the *Demiurge* — created this dark dimension of matter by creating separation from the Light.

This sub-universe of physical matter where mankind currently finds itself is really *Satan's* universe. Satan is the sole ruler of this physical realm of pain and suffering that exists within God's greater universe. Satan alone controls the fate of all souls trapped inside. He can punish or reward them depending on his whim, just as the God of the Abrahamic religions is wont to do. This is further evidence that the God known as Jehovah, Yahweh, and Allah is really Satan.

Satan wields his power through his archons — the fallen angels that were cast out of God's realm. These archons rule regions of the sub-universe on Satan's behalf. These beings are referred to in Genesis, the first book of the Bible, as *Nephilim*, or "Sons of God."

The *Nephilim* descended to Earth and founded a race called the *Anakim* by mixing their seed with man's through marriage. These entities introduced mankind to the occult arts of astrology, magic, and alchemy. The Illuminati claim to be descended from the *Nephilim*. The Sons of God conferred the Kabbalah, or Ancient Wisdom, upon them.

Satan's goal is to prevent humanity from seeing the Light and escaping his diabolical domain. He will use any tactic to keep the people in the dark and trapped in his sub-universe. He will appear to be charming, and offer riches, success, fame and sex to those who can be bribed. Those who cannot will be terrorized into bowing to his will. For example, he created the frightening image of himself as a fiery demon hurling the dammed into a blazing pit of fire to control people through fear.

Although Satan is Rex Mundi, "king of the world," *Abraxas* will assist those who seek Divine Light. Lucifer, the Bearer of Light, "fell" to Earth to share knowledge with mankind. The Illuminati believe that only Lucifer can save them from the dark power of Satan. They look to Lucifer to purge false religions and guide the human race to the one "true" religion, which is Luciferianism. The Illuminati believe that following Lucifer's light will lead one out of Satan's realm and into God's realm. By adhering to the wisdom of the eternal light and truth of Lucifer, the darkness can be vanquished.

This all seems fairly innocuous until it is discovered that the grandmasters use ancient rituals of King Solomon to invoke demonic entities called Djinn (aka Qareens) in "sacred" occult rituals. These entities are Satan's fallen angels or the *Nephilim*.

King Solomon had been introduced to Illuminism by a wandering mystic. The king founded the Order of Solomon dedicated to furthering the secret knowledge. The floor of the temple King Solomon constructed was adorned with the black and white checkerboard design. This recurring Illuminati theme symbolizes the interconnectedness of light and dark. However, it has a profound esoteric meaning beyond this.

The white square on the checkerboard represents the person, whereas the adjoining dark square represents his or her dark (evil) twin. This twin is a Djinn spirit. The Djinn shadows the person at all times, seeking any opportunity to exert its nefarious influence. The Illuminati hope to garner information about future events from these demonic spirits. They also cajole the Djinn into bestowing wealth and power upon the Illuminists. They conjure up these demons in secret rituals, such as the Merkaba Hexagram Ceremony.

Merkaba means "light spirit body," where *Mer* is light, *Ka* is spirit, and *Ba* is body. This energy field is the spirit body, and is surrounded by counter-rotating fields of light. These spirals of energy form DNA, and transport the human spirit body from one dimension to another.

The Merkaba Hexagram (aka the Star of David or the Seal of Solomon) is an inter-dimensional psychic vehicle. Illuminati grandmasters and the students at the higher levels use it to project their consciousness into a higher dimension. The Merkaba Hexagram is comprised of two equally sized interlocked tetrahedra of light. The two tetrahedra have a common center where one points up and the other points down. This point symmetry form is called a stella Octangula or stellated Octahedron and can be created by extending the faces of a regular octahedron until they intersect.

In the Merkaba Hexagram Ceremony, an out-of-body meditation is used to travel into an alternative inter-dimensional reality. The participant imagines the two stella Octangula as counter-rotating. He or she also uses special *prana* ("vital life") breathing techniques, certain eye movements, and chants *mantras* to create a saucer shaped energy field around his or her body. Once activated, this special energy field is capable of carrying one's consciousness directly into the higher dimensions.

Author, occultist, and Illuminati initiate, Israel Regardie, warned that the "Hexagrams of Saturn," as he called the double tetrahedra, are

> not for idle meditation use and is very much about an offering to the power of Saturn. I find it strange that the

Illuminati are using satanic rituals in their meditations, when they proclaim to be against the Demiurge, the one they call Satan.

Perhaps aware of the danger of invoking demons, King Solomon would summon a higher being of Light and a Djinn spirit simultaneously. Solomon called upon the Djinn to bestow knowledge, power, and riches upon him, but he knew he needed protection from it at the same time. The higher being of Light was there to shield him from the demonic entity, should it wish to inflict injury upon him.

Unfortunately, many members of the Illuminati who have played around with summoning demons have become merged with these beings. Some have even been outright possessed by them. The hapless Illuminist then basically serves as the human vehicle for the Djinn entity. The unsuspecting Illuminati spend the rest of their lives as slaves to the demons they have invited into their lives.

This leads to the ultimate goal of the Illuminati, which is the Externalization of the Luciferian Hierarchy. This sinister stratagem involves turning human beings into biological hosts for Satan's fallen angels. The *Nephilim* possess these human bodies and use them to live in this world. Author and theosophist, Alice A. Bailey, revealed that, "In later stages...senior Members of the Hierarchy will appear and take outer and recognizable physical control of world affairs."

The *Nephilim* will exploit the Illuminati to gain control of this world by hijacking their human bodies. Once the Djinn "walk the Earth," they will impose their draconian New World Order meritocracy upon the whole of humanity. Thus, the New World Order is literally an inhuman system devised by Satan's fallen angels to further control and enslave mankind. People will remain firmly under Satan's metaphorical thumb, if the Illuminati succeed in implementing their New World Order agenda.

▲

Conclusion

The Illuminati lure desired recruits to their Order by seducing them with the promise of learning secrets forbidden to others. The initiation process is structured so as to gradually transition the student from believing in God to abandoning Him for Lucifer. The Illuminati grandmasters are careful to conceal the fact that they worship Lucifer and invoke demons from the would-be Illuminists until the students have been mentally prepared to receive such information.

The first phase of indoctrination involves discrediting the Abrahamic religions, namely Judaism, Christianity, and Islam, because they reject Lucifer and venerate the *Demiurge*, who is masquerading as Yahweh, Jehovah, and Allah. Faith in the God of the Torah, Bible, and Koran must be destroyed before the student will accept Lucifer in His stead. The second phase entails establishing a more or less credible scientific basis for the Illuminati belief system. Finally, in the third phase of the initiation process, it is revealed that Lucifer is God, and that the Illuminati call upon demonic Djinn spirits to reveal secret knowledge to them and grant them earthly power, wealth, and influence.

As it turns out, these Djinn have their own agenda. These body-snatchers use humans as biological hosts to invade the Earth. Satan's fallen angels plan to reshape the world after their hostile takeover to their liking. Part of this restructuring involves imposing the oppressive New World Order meritocracy upon the people of the Earth. Under this system, everyone will be forced to follow the pagan Luciferian religion.

By revealing the information contained in a secret Illuminati manuscript entrusted to him, the author hopes to diminish the air of mystery that surrounds the Illuminati. Anyone who may be tempted by the appeal of secrecy will be able to read this book and discover what those secrets are. Now that the hidden agenda has been disclosed, each person can decide for him- or herself if he or she wishes to help Satan's archons usher in the New World Order and impose their "Golden Age" on the whole of humanity.

▲

<u>About the Author</u>

Michael Adair graduated college with a masters degree in computer science in 1984. He began to show an interest in secret fraternal societies as early as 1986. His discovery of the various methods used by world leaders to control and influence the populations of the world led him on a quest to learn more about their position on global politics. Through a series of contacts with the Knights Templar and the Knights of Malta, he was introduced to members of the Bavarian Illuminati. He soon discovered many important secrets of the global elite, and their plans to bring serious changes to the free nation states of the world. In his new book, Forbidden Secrets of the Illuminati, the author exposes the primary belief system of this mysterious group of aristocrats and political leaders, along with many dark secrets that are part of their fraternal order.